Last Water Song

BOOKS BY PATRICK LANE

Poems New and Selected (1978)

The Measure (1981)

Old Mother (1983)

A Linen Crow, a Caftan Magpie (1985)

Selected Poems (1987)

Milford & Me (children's poems, 1989)

Winter (1990)

Mortal Remains (1991)

How Do You Spell Beautiful? (short stories, 1992)

Too Spare, Too Fierce (1995)

Breathing Fire: Canada's New Poets (editor, with Lorna Crozier, 1995)

Selected Poems: 1977–1997 (1997)

The Bare Plum of Winter Rain (2000)

Addicted: Notes from the Belly of the Beast (editor, with Lorna Crozier, 2001)

Go Leaving Strange (2004)

Breathing Fire 2: Canada's New Poets (editor, with Lorna Crozier, 2004)

There is a Season (memoir, 2004)

Syllable of Stone (UK selected, 2006)

LAST WATER SONG

Patrick Lane

HARBOUR PUBLISHING

Harbour Publishing Co. Ltd.
P.O. Box 219
Madeira Park, BC
V0N 2H0
www.harbourpublishing.com

Cover: "The Last Work," Bloodline series by Drew Harris.
Some poems in this collection have previously appeared in *Geist* and the *Globe and Mail*.
Printed in Canada.

Harbour Publishing acknowledges financial support from the Government of Canada through the Book Publishing Industry Development Program and the Canada Council for the Arts, and from the Province of British Columbia through the British Columbia Arts Council and the Book Publisher's Tax Credit.

THE CANADA COUNCIL | LE CONSEIL DES ARTS
FOR THE ARTS | DU CANADA
SINCE 1957 | DEPUIS 1957

BRITISH
COLUMBIA
ARTS COUNCIL
Supported by the Province of British Columbia

Library and Archives Canada Cataloguing in Publication

Lane, Patrick, 1939–
    Last water song / Patrick Lane.

Poems.
ISBN 978-1-55017-450-2

    I. Title.
PS8523.A53L38 2007   C811'.54   C2007-903890-5

Dedicated to Lorna Crozier

"What luck, what luck to be loved . . ."
—*Irving Layton* ·

Contents

PART ONE

FOR RED LANE

When I left you on the side of the road after I kicked you out you were already practising your death, your cards laid down in Patience, that solitary game still in your mind. Jack of hearts on the queen of spades. Nine on the ten, two on the three . . . Christ, what do I remember? You stuffed your hands into worn pockets, your jacket bunched against the wind coming cold off the Nicola River, the wind out of the north, your red hair, the fear I understood and still can't name. Johnny knew it too. Brothers. I tried to find that road today, write now on my knees beside the dry hills where the pine trees reach for water. It was somewhere around here. Hell, the old road is gone and now there's nothing to hold on to. Your death was singing there in the gravel. It sang to you as a boy. You were always somewhere gone, your punishment the friends who loved you, no matter the loss. Brothers are strangers to the world, all blood and crazy laughter. Today I drove the new highway, pulled off into the dry stones where the river used to flow. I found a dead girl upcountry once, twenty miles east of Spences Bridge, but that was long ago. Right around here. The little cutthroat trout were lilting in her hair. Sometimes water is the last place you look to find a home. She was so lonely there and then the walk out, the telling what's become a story, the *where?* the *why?* the *how?* Like her, having nowhere to go, you went there anyway. *It's okay,* you said. *I'll see you later.* Both were lies, the truth just another kind of terror. Two months later you were gone. It's like the dead girl. Sometimes at night the bodies come back, if only to tell me what they couldn't say. I thought my life was mostly luck. Looking back, most of it seems bad. You thought I should stay in the north. *Never come out*, you said. You wrote me from Vancouver. I couldn't wait to leave. That was '63, a year before your death. The road was dust. I could barely see you looking back, the mills below, the burners spewing ashes into sky. Every few years I almost find a place where we had been. I drive down old roads, most of them changed. Trying to find the lost places I sometimes have to climb higher into the trees. The old gravel roads are all in pieces now. Remember driving Cat on the Rogers Pass? It was '58, I think. What do numbers mean? It was summer and there were so many mountains. We were pounding down the new highway. One time after work you took me up a creek to where a single pool gathered falling water. There was a doe drinking deep, her soft face delicate among the stones come down from mountains. I can see her now. There was always somewhere if we looked for it hard enough. That girl was beautiful, caught in the broken poplar limbs. O, your death's alive in me! Poets say love goes on after lovers die. But what of brothers? Was it you who stopped the darkness? Was it you who tried to save me? And Johnny? What of him? Who were we back in the days of the little boys? You're still somewhere, the pebbles and dust you touched with your worn boots. Was it here? The wind comes hard down the valley. It did that day. I think this place is where you hitched away. I think this is where I left you.

FOR ADELE WISEMAN

You were never a poet though you had their ways, the insular ego, the doubt of any worth. In China you drove me crazy with the books you'd brought packed in a cheap suitcase bound with rope. You always asked the men to help you get it on and off the bus. It weighed two hundred pounds. I think it was Xi'an when I told you that was it. The suitcase had broken open, books all over the road and you, the tough little Winnipeg girl, obdurate as always, insisting the books travel all the way to dissident writers. I passed them out to people passing by. You stood there on your stocky peasant legs that might've held up a world if you'd found one. You were never confused, only confounded. For me it was always the other way around. Who knows where your words are now? I never understood the shame. How to explain the time I dropped my fork at the table and leaned down to get it? Everyone had left the kitchen by then, just you and me left. I knew there was something wrong, could read it in your face. You sat there staring at a place made from first causes. When I picked up the fork I looked at you below the table. Blood dripped off your stool into a pool on the floor. Your bright life fell like thick water. I called a friend and then an ambulance. A crazy house. In the bedroom off the living room Betty lay feigning a heart attack while she waited for the night and his hand to creep between her legs. *He comes at night and kneels beside the bed*, she said. I thought at first she was afraid and then she said, *It's so exciting.* I couldn't wait to go. What a zoo. And yet I think I only see the surfaces of things. I'd like to see more but desire is never satisfied. You dug holes in your books, filled them with emptiness and reasons. A little girl from Winnipeg with tears. You kept your secrets close. I loved your words and taught them to the young. They seemed to understand. Seemed, not did. The young never know anything. It's the trouble with immortality. It doesn't understand everything hurts eventually. I know, I was taught hard by women like you. The war got in the way of things like love. I think if there'd been a man when I was young I'd have learned women were mortal, creatures of the world, but women taught me and they taught me wrong. Like you, their surfaces shone so bright I couldn't see beyond the sheen to the ordinary world they lived in. It's not blame I'm looking for. Surrender is something a life needs if only to get by. The pool of blood was just another mystery to me. The old first-aid man in me came out and my first thought was to stop the blood, but how staunch the look on your face? First aid always stops short of burdens. It never lasts. There was something I wanted to ask you but I've forgotten now. It doesn't matter. Questions are the answers we already know, so if I've forgotten it's because the need has gone with you back to that street in Winnipeg, the little girl on sturdy legs who had to look after so much she forgot about herself. Maybe that kind of forgetting is denial, a wish to push the pain into someone else's life. Maybe that was me too, there on the floor with a dishtowel between your legs, the bright blood tarnished black by a medium it didn't understand. I mean this world, and so did you.

FOR AL PITTMAN

With you Newfoundlanders, everything came down to the sea except your father's boat. It ended in a field rotting in the sun after he died, you sitting in the wheelhouse with your bottle, staring across the withered summer grass, both of us drunk. You told me through tears of the outports and the years. What I remember is the withering of it all, that boat pulled out of the water, the hull dry, the cabin windows broken. You tried to turn the wheel but it was frozen by the sun, rusted out by weather. It was like you to be running rough water on land, the right tears in the wrong place. All those years. We could both find a metaphor in that now, or I could, now you're gone. The last time I saw you, you were hunched over your drink in the bar in Corner Brook and couldn't be moved by words, told me to leave you alone. The bartender shrugged. There were too many echoes for me. I thought of all the poets I saw die with their hands clenched around a glass or puking booze and blood into a toilet bowl; the years I tried to drown, the bottles as empty as the times. Christ, we went back a long way. I think it was '67 we met, you in Montreal, and me the first time in the East. Did we fight? Probably. You Newfies are always troublesome, proud and vulnerable, with your gift for the insult of love, the tenderness of hate. I thought your wife a pretty one and likely made a pass at her. Those days I wasn't much good for anything but trouble, and poetry. It was the same with you. The many times together, the night you locked yourself out of our house in Regina and got lost in the dawn alley as you searched for a cigarette butt to light. That you were naked but for your underwear made little sense to the kindly neighbour woman who guided you back. You passed out on a lawn chair. When I found you hours later you were sunburned to a salmon. I think it was the only time your skin was ever touched by the sky. Jesus, Al, I loved you but I couldn't bear the dying, the steady day and nightness of it. I was dying too, but that doesn't mean much now. I'm still dying, just more slowly. We were always drunk together, Al. Always, with Nowlan or Newlove or Acorn, or whomever happened to be around, strangers like ourselves. I remember guiding you off the stage in Vancouver. The audience was laughing at you, your wandering jokes and stories. I knew you were dying up there, that you'd got lost and couldn't find your way back. I put my arm around you and you whispered in my ear, *Thank Christ*, and then you asked, *Where are we?* I still don't have an answer. Some questions leave me reeling. Maybe where we were was in a boat in a dry field far from the sea. Maybe that was the best we had together. If I close my lids I can see you in the red light the sun makes of my eyes. You're up there at the wheel with a good sea and a fair wind. Someone's laughing – your father, me – and we're heading into harbour, the light falling across a Canada far to the west, and there's a life to be led on the waters, in a dry field, with no one to hurt us, and tears enough to go around.

FOR AL PURDY

It wasn't the brawling man who wrote of *dangerous women with whiskey-coloured eyes*, it was the other man I knew in '62, the awkward one you hid inside the Contact book, the one who spoke of lines that never end. That's what I heard first and that's the man I knew. It was the uneasiness you had with the myth you'd made of yourself. You were a mama's boy and spoiled like only-children are. Even your ride on the freight train back in the thirties wasn't a real struggle, was more adventure than endurance. Survival had nothing to do with it, though later you'd learn, picking through Air Force garbage with Eurithe to keep food on the table. Three days in Vancouver and you couldn't wait to hop a freight back to Ontario, homesick, a little scared. Suffering was never your strong point. It took Eurithe to help you with that. But I remember '66, the night we left the Cecil to visit Newlove on Yew Street and giddy with drink I threw a full bottle of beer at the sky. You stopped dead and waited till the bottle fell and smashed. *Only throw empty bottles at the moon*, you said, shaking your head at the waste of a drink. It's a metaphor I've lived with in this life, that moon. Or the time we stole books at the McStew Launch in '73. You told me to stop taking the poetry. *Take the picture books*, you said. *No one will give you money for a poem.* Jack McClelland was railing at us and Newlove was dancing drunk on a table while Farley glowered in a corner because he wasn't the centre of attention. Clarkson was prissy and Layton was trying once again to get laid. God knows where Acorn was. All names now, men and women either dead or getting closer. And you? I could talk with you about the attributes of *Rubus spectabilis* and Etruscan tombs. We could go from there to a discussion about the relative venom of *Laticauda colubrina*. You liked the leaps and made a poetry from space. You went from the yellow-lipped sea krait to the eyes of Eurithe and found love at the end of your complaint. I think love was at the heart of all you did, the only loss you knew. Not knowing what you should learn, you learned everything. An autodidact (I loved that word when I was young, it gave my ignorance a name) you put in everything you could, your mind moving like your body, a poem too big to fit into the world. Sitting at the kitchen table three months before your death you told me you'd never had a friend. *Are you my friend?* you asked. I'll never forget your eyes. There were never any cheap tricks in your art. It's the one thing you taught me. Don't tell it slant you might've said. Your poems were Möbius strips. Following your mind was like my wandering in South America years ago. I knew there was no end, it was the going I had to learn, the nowhere we all get to. I split the word these days.

Right now I'm here. You liked the story of me almost dying from a centipede sting in the jungle east of Ecuador, the little brown woman who nursed me back to life as she fed me soup made from boiled *cuy*. Like most men you liked stories. All your confessions were metaphors, those tired horses in the dust at Hundred Mile the measure. Or the time you made coffee in the frying pan in Toronto for Lorna and me, the bubbles of bacon grease just something to add body to the day. With you I could almost make it through. I fixed your deathbed, the second-hand one you and Eurithe bought at a garage sale. You stood in a reel while I hammered it together. Three days later you were gone. I could say I still have words but none of them add up to you. Whispers mostly in the racket. Poems go round and round, this one too, never quite getting there, but I still live, and your *ivory thought* is all that keeps me warm some nights, still writing, still alive. It's a cheap out, Al, but where else to go but back to you grabbing the picture books, telling me once again that poems don't sell. They never did.

FOR ALDEN NOWLAN

There's a dark river in both our lives and poverty not always of the spirit but the flesh. The cold waters drag the salmon to their deaths in the great pools up the Miramichi. Those born in forests know what shadows are. I always imagined you walking a dirt road, me behind you, writing down the details of your life, the footsteps you thought would lead your body out. No mention of the soul. There is no common usage for that word. It's one we've lost or if not lost then buried under the porch planks of the shacks we grew up in. Still, I see you walking down that road wearing the clean shirt your mother ironed for you, the collar turned and the sleeves shortened. Something handed down like the stories of Culloden and Ypres. "Bannon Brook" still catches at me, that bobcat coming wild through the smokescreen of your words. I watched the pages roll out when I printed *The Jesus Game* in Trumansburg, your poems laying themselves down. I bound them. Now, my copy barely holds its cover. I was never much good at permanence. My hands have opened your poems so many times and now my hands are worn just like the paper. Things slip away into the gentleness big men know. Touching anyone could hurt them. I'm not sure whom the pronoun refers to now, you or sweet Claudine. Her and Johnny. We always drank too much whenever we met. There was always a party, Ray and David, Louis and Al, the young men who worshipped you. Only David escaped, though he carries the old scar deep in the ball of his thumb. It's the hook his country left. You never fished for anything but poems. Your Nancy searched the roads for you but you had left by then, gone down to the city. You waited for her in the poems, half-afraid she'd read herself into your life. The last time I saw you it was two months from silence. It took ten minutes to find your way from the sleeping room upstairs to the living room below. I could hear your body smack the walls as you blundered drunk to see me. It sounded like someone slapping the belly of a dying cod. Claudine was bright and beautiful as she served me beer. *He'll be down in a minute*, she said and chatted the years I'd come and gone. You sat there with your orangutan face so swollen I barely knew you. It would be easy to say the moose was you, mysterious, naked, come down from the hills to die, but things are never that easy. I've tried to write this letter twice before. Maybe I'll get it right this time. You raged at me the night we met in '67. You made me an honorary Maritimer at ten. At two in the morning you stripped the gift away, cursing me for being from the West. We almost came to blows, you swinging the empty gin bottle and me trying hard not to spill my whiskey, ducking out the door for a cigarette with a girl I didn't know, but for her mouth and her tumbled hair. Like Purdy, you were our love poet. No one can touch your tenderness. It was like you were ashamed of what you wanted most, no one listening to your whispered, gentle words. Do we ever escape the past, Alden? Tell me if you know. I keep walking behind that kid on the dirt road, the one with the ironed shirt and the gumboots. I never catch up, but I know that's what the dream is all about. It's enough I keep walking knowing nothing changes and only the details hold. It's the way things are that matter, nothing altered, the boots leaving their scuff in the mud, the clouds coming hard out of Maine, and the fists of the boy swinging in the cold wind of that rocky country as he goes down the river, full of anger and something he thinks is love. Despair when you're young is always taken wrong. You knew that in "Pimlico," the flow of those dark waters leading you up, not out. It's why we go where we go, the Ithaca at the end of a Cavafy poem, everything we need on the journey that takes us home.

FOR ANNE SZUMIGALSKI

In the bar at Fort Qu'Appelle we danced country and western, a couple of Cree or Sioux guitars and a white man on the drums. The beer glasses rattled on the tables while Hank Snow rose from his grave to sing our hearts. You were so huge, your dewlapped flesh white mountains in that lake-locked cut of land down from the old asylum where plains poetry began. You floated cross the floor. The farmers and cowboys gaped as you twirled light as a red fox angel, your dip and weave as much invention as my own imagining. I loved you best in my arms, your smile the wicked grin of the bad little girl you were. I used to dream of being buried in your flesh. I always asked why you never wrote of the war. You nursed the bone racks from the concentration camps when you were a girl. It seems a century ago now. You took the first workshop I ever led in '76 in Saskatoon. I remember saying there was a problem with your poem about a girl giving birth to a fox. The middle was all wrong. You argued with me, your eyes telling me you'd wanted praise, not blame. I'd never heard of you. Then you sent me your book, *Woman Reading in Bath*. I read it that winter. You were a poet. But you never did get the fox poem right. The next spring on the Sunshine Coast I sat under my old cedar tree down by the tumbled stones. She was the one I prayed to when I left that marriage. Old Cedar Mother. The man who bought the land cut her down. I think grief rises from neglect, the wish to save a part of the life you leave. I never wanted to save you, but I still grieve for that tree. She was always there for me. The strangest part of you was your desire for acolytes. You loved their loving you, their admiration, and more, their hopefulness. Like the ghosts that summer. You came late to Fort Qu'Appelle. How you missed talking to the dead. Your daughter, Kate, and I called up a ghost from the Ouija board. I thought I was going to die but the ghost didn't want me. I'd just come back from China, tired and spent, full of temples and tragedy. I needed ghosts that year. I don't know where I'm going here. There was a misery in you, a shard of ego stuck in your bright eyes. I always thought you went wrong when you started searching for a place that would admire you. I loved your first poems best, your garden too. And the loneliness. You carried England like a bag lady carries rags. Story was the thing you trusted least. Your lyrics thought too much. But, O, Anne, how you danced! Up on your toes you'd cross the floor like the tiniest angel, the one who stood first on the holy pin and danced all heaven to her perch. I think your body took the life you should've had. A prima ballerina lived in you. And that sounds like your poems were something less. And that's not true. Like the cowboy songs Hank Snow wrote that weren't meant for cattle drives, your poems kept trying. It's all a matter of tone, the way you spoke your world, not what you said but how you said it rearranged. Mostly I remember the time of the ghosts at Fort Qu'Appelle, you and I walking down by the lake and you telling me of the war years, the men who died in your hands, your Polish man, the eccentric little girl who had no friends but the ones she imagined. They were who you wrote for. There's room for everyone on the head of a pin. Just come, you said. I did and that's how I danced you, red fox angel, you.

FOR BRONWEN WALLACE

Your poems are stories with common bones, cadence the guide that turns a people into a map of your heart, a history made from prison stones, everything in the details, letters that asked for grace and caught it with the lifelines you threw out. We sat out on the lawn back of the house in Saskatoon, you with your joint and a beer in the other hand. I used to wonder how you could make sense stoned. I never could. Two tokes and I'd be under the bed hiding in a corner like a dustball afraid of a broom. My world was cocaine and whiskey. I could ask how *I* made sense. I don't think I ever did. You just kept on talking about the women you knew, the ones in prison, the ones just dead, the ones who were your friends. All that fragility, the blown glass ornaments that were their lives, you juggling them in the wind, trying hard not to let them fall. I liked your anger and your stubbornness, the way you'd tense your jaw as if you had to worry something in there, some hard candy heart that wouldn't melt. But all the struggle never gave me you. You kept your tears for poems. Back in the League days you were always tied up with Mary, Roo, and Carolyn. There wasn't room for a man. I kept my distance, watched your feminist moves, and danced what steps I knew in the suites where men punched each other out or got left in gutters, too drunk to understand your voice, your quiet rage. It was the common plight of men who misplaced love, thinking change could be made with a boyish plea for mercy. You'd seen enough of that, a beer bottle smashed against a wall, a woman beaten by the man who loved her. *There's only so much anyone can say*—or do. This learning to love is hard and common magic is mostly shared on sidewalks where the furniture gets piled, in safe houses where a woman finds what love there is among her kind before going back to the storm. What I loved most about you was forgiveness and your need to find a common truth in a common touch. And maybe that's it, a touch and nothing more. I wasn't around when the cancer ate your mouth. I hated my thinking it was ironic a poet could die in the place where words were made. How cheap a borrowed pain in the limits a body is. Rooms within rooms, a lawn and a man and woman talking about Levine and Wayman, Purdy and Acorn, the men you said had given you a place where you could cry the time. Neruda too. And Lowther. It was the fists of men, the women bruised and broken, the indignities that dogged you. But who was it I knew when I knew you? Facts get mixed up in poems and fictions are a poet's safest bet to change a world. You were all stories, beginnings, middles, ends, and the means was in the measure you ladled out. You said, *we carry our lives in our hands*, and we do, an open hand held out to hold another, simple things so fragile even a breath can break them, a word, a poem, *the cadence in a woman's voice,* like a rocking chair someone's left. It moves by itself a while, then stops, like a tree fallen in a forest no one hears.

FOR EARLE BIRNEY

It was words like *skree* that got me, *pika*, *grizzly*, creatures I'd never seen before in poems, the Rockies, lands I'd walked and mountains that were not a problem, mine nor yours, until you told me so, the *otter rocks* then changed, and what I knew was what I'd lost, childhood and the wilderness both foreign lands where I had to learn there was a trance called men. Or maybe just a man. There was that party at Livesay's house in '66 when you made a pass at my wife. You weren't the first and wouldn't be the last. I hardly noticed, my life already moving past her into what I didn't know. You wrote me back in '62 and told me to keep writing. I was up north, a first-aid man in a dead-end milltown, nursing the dregs of cheap whiskey, tapping out poems about bears at burning barrels, a cougar at the door, a man with his hand cut off, ordinary things in the tired nights when my children slept and my wife had given up on me. Strange how I thought you were already dead, but that's how it was back then, the only poets I knew long gone, their ghosts looking down off Westminster Bridge, words from another country. You said: *no man sees where the trout lie now.* I missed the first two lines. It took years for me to find the lady. These lines, long and wandering, are how I knew you. Poetry is a different kind of slowness, the break in things taking forever to happen. I remember sitting in Lionel's room and listening to you talk about Trotsky when you were his secretary. History was always just around the corner with you. *I am my own clown*, you said, and now I think I understand, for every clown has a sad face under the mask. That's why they frighten us so when we're still young enough to believe that nothing can save us from the dark myth we can't be severed from no matter our trying. I think that's why we make a past from ourselves. When we're far away the only truths we have are inhuman. It's funny, Earle, how much you mattered then. I never thought I learned from you, yet tonight I read "El Greco: Espolio" and think I got my carpenter poem from you. Lines live in poets. You wait long enough and everything you've read gets said again. The father of a poem is what you write. Still, with the creek outside my trailer door purling, the wind in the fir trees, and me a little tired staring down at the river David Thompson never saw, the one Simon Fraser named for him, I hear the black bear rummaging among the burned pork-chop bones, the green bread crusts, the rotting bits of food in the ashes, and think how near a few words can take us to another time. I stopped reading you back in the early seventies. I'd grown tired of local masters. I think it was the old contempt for what is known. I needed an imagined master, not the one I knew. That's where the quest began, I guess, that looking everywhere else for what I'd already found. In this early book of yours I read today, some student's written under "The Road to Nijmegen," *War memorials are synechdoche for people*. Yeah, I know it's spelled wrong, and the poem isn't about war memorials anyway, yet I know my father's friend was burned alive in his tank on the salient near Caen. Maybe that's it, I don't know. Like most letters to the dead, this one's gone too long. Like the lines, it's wandering. It was words that started me. There's no easy end to them: *pika, grizzly, otter, ice.*

FOR ELIZABETH SMART

Where were we? Cambridge? That ancient city I'd read about in books. Peggy and Graeme went off to punt the Cam. They were tired of ghost stories. Seán disappeared in some woman's arms and I was left wandering. The romance of the place wore thin by nightfall, drunk as I was, the cocaine mostly gone, the hours bottoming, and me drifting through a party. All those English voices a little shrill, a little brittle, the women edgy, so that I wondered at my father saying years ago there was no better place to take your leave. Those English women, he said, were the wildest in Europe. But those were the war years. I think peace made them elegant, their irony a game. Too many buttons. I ended up a little lost sitting halfway down the stairs, or was it halfway up. You sat down beside me and we talked. I'd read your *Opus Dei* the year before. Back in North America they thought you the perfect victim, you and Sylvia. Funny how you both went crazy for English poets. What was it about George you loved? When we met Barker at the pub that day he introduced his new wife to me, saying, *This is my latest cunt.* You simpered, your voice a wheedle, while the wife smiled and said, *Oh George.* He sent her for another jug of beer and then spit on your breasts. You never moved. He laughed at you, your servility and worship more than he could bear. It was me got you back to Canada. That was a mistake. You said it would be, said you didn't think it right for you. I should've listened, but what the hell? You came to Regina for Christmas that year. I knew you were alone and thought it would be nice to be with someone for the holiday. You said you'd stay two days. I told you five. *I'm not usually good after two days*, you said. I insisted five. And what a bad little girl you were. On the third night I carried you to bed and laid you down. You were so drunk. You grabbed me and pulled me on top of you. *Suck my tits*, you said. *Please fuck me.* I covered you, then stroked your head as if you were a fevered child, a nightmare. Both are right. You were best suited to a village pub. A city like Edmonton was like the moon to you, that bifurcated city without a heart. I liked your silliness, the clever little girl you were, not woman. And your garden back in England, the wildness of it, flowers everywhere awry, so that to walk into it you could get lost in the dizzy planting you made of love. Then the year in Toronto the Ugly, the nights you sat in the doughnut shop on Bloor and talked to the street people till the dawn came up on the Annex and you could stagger home. I remember your breasts when you pulled your blouse open, my fumbling as I tried to cover them, a bit ashamed for you. George ate you alive but you were a willing feast. He used and discarded you like an empty bottle in a ditch. There's no forgiving him, but why you kept going back I'll never know. And he was a minor poet at best. So English. How you loved your liquor. I didn't know that ten years later I'd be as bad as you. Strange how things can haunt you. I liked *Rogues and Rascals* best. It was more like you, scattered, witty and bright. The words were like your hair when you'd brush it back, drunk, the wet blonde locks falling forward again as you slurred your way to another bit of praise for Barker. You were the poet, not him. I can see you in California walking the dusty trail and wanting him. All he wanted was your money. Fucking you was just a way to get it. Still, I don't blame him. It takes two to make a tragedy out of love. He was crude and coarse, a brutal man in love with hurting women. You were both caricatures, excessive and obsessed. You out-romanticized him. I think I liked you best on the stairs back there in Cambridge, two Canucks for a moment lost in an old Empire, laughing our way through a bottle of cheap scotch, you saying, *Canada might be nice.* It was, but you were never good at nice. I wish there'd been another time for us, but that's wishful and foolish, silly of me now. I was never good with victims, no man is, not with the willing kind. How you stood the English I'll never know. Like every city in the world I've ever been, I couldn't wait to get back home, but that's the country boy in me. I remember stroking your forehead, your eyes closing, your sleep at last, and me rising from my knees beside the bed and going to my woman, one who'd left her childhood behind, someone I could hold in the grown-up world I wished you knew.

FOR FRANK SCOTT

Sometimes you stand in the concourse of Central Station in downtown Montreal unsure of where to go and see a man with white hair and a topcoat open to the wind he left outside, a man hurrying across the marble floor, his arms wrapped tight around a briefcase hugged to his narrow chest. It's an old guy but in this city of strangers who speak another tongue you recognize him and as he goes by you catch his arm. He spins to a stop, turning once around like a child's toy. It was you, of course, and we stood there in the place where people come and go, no one staying around for the long haul, the ones arriving looking tired, the ones leaving looking worried as if the place they were going to wouldn't know them. A long story, Frank, but it was your glee when you told me what you had in the briefcase. A little boy clutching to his chest the first draft of the founding of the CCF in Winnipeg. You'd been rummaging in boxes up in your attic and found the notes and the first rough copy you'd made when you were secretary to the men who made us almost human. You were off to Ottawa to give it to the National Archives. *I'd forgotten I had it*, you said. *Imagine that?* I nodded yes, but meant no. You were too much history for me, your battles so much a myth I thought they'd all been won and we were safe. When was that, '73 or '74? I don't remember, it's all too long ago, but I do still see you holding this country to your chest, the smile on your face when you let me touch the pages. It was like some holy thing, as much a part of me as the Magna Carta is to Brits. You never had the common touch. Like your father you spoke to people, then seemed to listen. You were too easily distracted by ideas to be a good poet. Your dreams turned into action, something poets never do. I loved your loves, the women you had, the brightest and the best, Phyllis and Pat, Betty and the rest. Only they can say what they found in you. You never stayed with anyone too long except your wife. That was the minister's son in you, wild enough for sin, but safe from temptation in the end. The image I have of you is the one in Saskatoon. It was the early eighties, a League of Poets meeting, one of the last you came to. Lorna and I were walking under the moon by the Saskatchewan River. We were watching the prairie flow by under the bridges, the sleeping hulls of pelicans floating in the eddies. You were sitting on a bench holding hands with a beautiful woman, an old lover you'd had back in those other years – the two of you under the old moon without a wish. I think the sight will hold me in the end. I count on that and never get past two. If there's a difference between you and me, it's that I always knew what a gift was and never confused love with duty. I think you did. For you the women were like what a man might find in war, someone you could make a promise to knowing your train left in the morning. You were always surprised they fell in love with you. That's the art of the con. The artist has to believe it at the time or it doesn't work. There's another difference, the part about history where I always failed at carrying through with the affairs of men. It's what you were best at. That and the changing, changeless face of the moon.

FOR GWENDOLYN MacEWEN

I was teaching "Dark Pines Under Water" today and now it's almost too late to wonder what anything means. I used to think I understood, but everything's imperfect, mostly us. Isn't that what you taught us? A *close reading* is what this teaching's called, students lowering their hands up to their wrists in your dark, imagined lake, the numbness that comes so quickly in February, the ice broken and the body learning what cold can do to the mind. To them they were only words, me too, without the *lonely*. Remember the time we sat in your apartment drinking scotch and talking about the poets and their poems? You kept brushing a lock of hair away from your eyes. I loved your laughter. Me? I had nowhere to go again, slept on your floor. It was Toronto, back in the day. I loved that you let me sleep alone. I paid for my beds back then, the one you gave me free. Late, we talked about Lawrence and his *Seven Pillars of Wisdom*, his years in the desert, his sordid soul in ruins. Your "Manzini." I keep going back to him. Like all good poems he offers no escape beyond the listening, beyond the circle your words draw around me still. This computer keeps telling me I'm doing things wrong. It draws coloured lines under the fragments, tells me there's no *u* in colour, no structure to my lines. It says there's no Manzini. Perhaps there isn't except in poems, circuses and sideshows, the tattooed man, the bearded lady, the dwarf, the albino, the freaks I loved when I was a boy. You loved them too. How you laughed when I told you the story of the lady with the goiter I followed when I was a child and how she stopped and let me reach up to touch that growth that hung from her, that pendulant bag of flesh. I was seven years old and thought beauty was the suffering you gave to little boys. I think you thought Lawrence was a man. How strange a woman's thinking is. When I was in my last room trying to swallow a mouthful of blood I thought of you, the bottle of vodka almost gone, morning coming on, sleep the only thing I could imagine, the kind of sleep only the dead drunk knows, the dreaming so terrible there is nothing to remember no matter how far down you reach. The closer I get to your poems the worse I feel. My students try, but there's no telling them they have to go deeper than their wrists in dark water. I remember so little now, Gwen. *Listen, there was this boy . . .*

FOR JOHN NEWLOVE

I lost the epitaph I wrote for you years ago. Strange how things have a way of coming true. It's as if everything has a way of getting to the end, the lies, how you balanced truth on the end of your pen. Did you wait long enough? Spare words from you would arrive and I would read through them to what silences there were. What to say? O, say nothing. You told me to listen to the snow, the misery in the sound of the wind as you looked for that *tired, halting song*. I think everything becomes a story in the end. You would have muttered about loneliness at that. I still have your baseball bat, the one you kept by the door in Regina in case the Indians came for you. It's a child's bat, chipped and scarred, as if you practised with it by hitting furniture pretending to a bravery you didn't think you had. But what good does that image do? I keep it by my front door in memory of you. If they ever come for me I'll let them have it. Memories like that don't do much good and stories are only things I tell my students to amuse them. *Did you really know John Newlove?* Did, not do. The better answer is probably, no. Imperfect flowers are the best we get. They die a little, watching us from the bookcase. Maybe that's what beauty is, fear at night, the cold, the diminishing hills, what must be done to endure. What must be done, John? Is it to write the old poem again, speak words in the tired arrangements, knowing the aridity, dead branches, imperfect flowers? You tied a yellow one to the carriage of your typewriter so its false petals would remind you of elusive lies. Things keep getting taken away, people, poems, the words we both got tangled up in. Hell, I keep getting tangled up in the tenses, past and present, the future imperfect. You told me once you learned a trick from Creeley and so dismissed your poems. But you always diminished your art. It was a kind of self-loathing, the one without definition, the one the philosophers go on about, thinking the perfect is attainable, that negative dialectic leading us to believe in nothing at the end. I published "White Lies" years ago, mimeographed it up in Vernon at a lawyer's office. They lent me their Gestetner for free, amazed a poet needed them. Do you remember the little white cards you wrote on in a script so tight even Ondaatje couldn't read it, so small you could cram a thousand words on a page? They were the notes to books you'd read, the histories, *the facts of this land* and its people, the explorers and the Indians, the men who had been gallant in their time, heroes so perfectly lonely in their quests. Gentleman John, they called you in your white shirts and shiny shoes. One night you called me drunk from Ottawa, told me your suit cost a thousand dollars. That's all you wanted me to know. And the day in the Plains Hotel when you spit in my face. You were so afraid, wanting only to be alone with your glass of gin and tonic with a twist. Ah, John, what's the use of going on? The poem reels out in its long, uneven dance. I miss you. But then, I miss Acorn and MacEwen too. You were all drunks. I miss me too at times. Does that make sense? Today I feel I'm just filling up a page and nothing is being said. Strange how I lost your epitaph. It was about the Spartans at Thermopylae, their combing their hair and you picking up the broken combs, selling them at a loss in the markets of Asia. Something like that. I think it was better years ago. I think all I have to hold onto are imperfect flowers. I can hold onto them, I think. It's easy enough to do. As you said once somewhere, weeds are flowers too.

FOR MILTON ACORN

Today I'm under the Seawall at English Bay where we both fell asleep
drunk under the sun after watching swallows chase a feather, the birds
passing it one to the other in a game of catch. The crows watched us
from under their helmets, almost amused, dark centurions waiting for
the inevitable slaughter, the barbarians come down from the trees, Chaka
and his warriors with their spears, all the history you raged about, the
inequalities, the people's needs. I think of you in my kitchen eating pea-
nut butter, gouging it out of the jar with your fingers, eating it in gouts.
My kids loved you for that, a man like a child, breaking rules they always
knew were wrong. They called you Uncle Miltie. Is that where everything
began? You were dried out three days from triple sec, sleeping on the
couch in my living room, me piecing out your Percodans and Valium
one at a time to keep you almost sane. There was no talk of the night I
washed the shit off your body, the filth a thick cake on your thighs, and
you screaming Gwen's name and my brother's. I loved your loves, but
hated your crying so. Poems stumble sometimes. Yet there are times they
catch at us much as swallows do feathers, in the air, the feather almost but
never falling. I sit down by a piece of driftwood and remember us sitting
against the same Seawall back in '65, you weeping over my brother, Red,
his early death. It was strange how you never thought I felt anything. I
cry too, but at other, simple things, a scarred stone in the sea, the tide
baring its dark shoulders, swallows in the air as much a god's calligra-
phy as birds, my tired hands. Bright warriors, I called them once. My
father liked you, perhaps because you'd been in his war. Who knows? I
think you tripped going up the gangplank in Halifax, hurt your head, and
by the time you got to England were sent home a little worse for wear.
Shaughnessy Hospital looked after you, a veteran you said, but the psy-
chiatrist told me quietly it was because you were a poet. *It's why we give
him the pension. Poems, you know.* I remember the ones you wrote on my
porch, "The Natural History of Elephants." Hell, the stink of your cheap
Cuban cigars, your muttered arguments and the rages against those who

betrayed you, Trotskyites, Marxist-Leninists, Stalinists, all the sad, petty miseries of your leftover thirties life. They still don't read you, Milton, though I've tried to change that. Little things, a poem as small as an elephant, as large as your heart. Today I'm trying to find a piece of myself I lost. Instead I find you. And the birds, of course, the swallows gone into the mist lifting from the wrack, the crows in their infinite patience, strutting at the edge of sea and land, an old one slightly tattered in his mourning cloak turning a crab shell in the hope of a meal. It makes me think of you at the White Lunch down on Hastings Street. Sometimes I find what I'm looking for, but it's never what I wish. Getting older is like that, things creep in, a memory, your tears, the tired flesh clean at last of shit, the rags I washed you with thrown from the window onto Fourth Street, their falling like smudged bodies into the gutter. Sometimes it's like that, the times I remember, you telling me I'd never be as good a poet as my brother, and loving you anyway as best I could, the sea all around us, and the crows like dark children, never quite believing you.

FOR ROY LOWTHER

1.

I could ask the old question, but I know there's no answer to why a man carries a hammer to his wife's room and bludgeons her to death. Maybe it's not an answer I'm looking for. A question, perhaps. One night back in '65 bissett and I went up your house to talk poetry. Milton Acorn told us about you, a communist, a man who believed in the worker. When I met you I saw a man who'd never worked hard in his life, just talked about it. Neither of us had heard of Pat and then in the middle of a boring night she read three poems. She was so beautiful, so young, her girls just babies, her poems full-grown and shining. I knew it was the first true woman's voice I'd ever heard and knew she was a poet. But you, Roy, with your pomp and bluster, put her down, dismissed her verse, telling her to be quiet and listen to him. It was too late for silence, Roy, too late for listening. One night last year I went to where you used to live and stood on the sidewalk as two children played on the lawn and wondered if their parents knew what happened in their home so many years ago. I hope they don't. Who needs to sleep in a house of blood? I remember you raging on the phone, telling me you'd kill her if she dared to read to the ironworkers at the hall. *She's got all the rest*, you said. *She's got no right to take my only audience away from me.* All that jealousy and rage, all that self-pity, that misery of the male when he has no power left. You used to lord it over her, that girl from North Vancouver, the shy one you controlled, the one you said you taught to write. You spoke of her as if she'd been a monkey in a cage. She was almost free of you.

2.

I think it's time I learned how to forgive you, think I've carried things long enough. Like the Carrier Indians of the North, I've packed Pat's ashes from Prince Rupert to Isla Negra, from Furry Creek to the Finger Lakes to Firenze and while there were times I put them down in fury or futility I always found them on my back the next go-round. Christ, why did you have to kill her? What reason did you have? Roy, that's where I always got it wrong, there being no *reason* at all in what you did. I've never killed anyone. I've used my fists to beat strangers in anger and once a friend out of love, and once I used a knife, but the guy didn't die and two months later we found ourselves in the same bar laughing over beer and counting his stitches. I've carried the wounded down mountain roads I travelled at night so I could see another's headlights coming on the hairpin curves. And I've buried friends, my mother, father, brother, children, hell, death seems to be most of life when I look back, the graves so many. What's an elegy for? I should be writing in distichs with hexameter my drum to carry words into song and sorrow. I should be a better poet. Sorrow is never long enough for me. Like a dog I keep going back to my own vomit, circling on a wound I can never find. There's that thing called *phantom pain*. Maybe that's what I have. In the end there are two deaths and I lie between the two of you like some child who doesn't understand the dark is everywhere.

FOR PAT LOWTHER

I almost forgot you. It was as if your dying wasn't a death, as if my refusal was the kind of mourning only water understands, its long falling and the wait before it becomes what it was, quiet and flowing, how I hide what grief there is. I never expected you to live. How many times did I beg you to leave the man who killed you and how many times did you refuse? You never said I didn't understand, you just said no. Yours was a different kind of death. Two days before Roy put the hammer to your skull he told me you'd no right to take the workers away from him. *She's got everyone else*, he said. All that anger because you were going to read with Trower and me at the Ironworkers Hall. Old history, him saying he'd kill you unless he read there too and me saying there was nothing I could do about the reading. Strange how simple language is and how we never think it real. To be murdered over poetry. I remember Roy running across your kitchen and smashing his head against the wall, Acorn coming up from his basement hole, watching in the hall as he chewed on his cigar, then you holding Roy, his broken head, his wretched self-pity, and you telling me you couldn't leave him, saying, *Look at this blood*. Today I read your early poems, the ones I published years ago, your chant, the one that begins with the lines, *Hands are beautiful things/ grasping a hammer . . .* your world *more precious and terrible* than I made sense of then. What's love but addiction. Pain too. I've known them both and know there's no leaving anyone or anything until you kill something in yourself. It's odd how tired a cliché is until you stare at it a while. You've got to live with words so long they come back new. It's like falling in a dream, the never landing part. They say if you land the heart breaks. It's too easy to read in poems what we want to find, the prophetic reduced to easy choices, "Kitchen Murder," the false biography the future makes of the past. What I hold on to are the years. Back in the early sixties you thought promise wasn't forbidden. Now you lie with the others *under the scalpelled earth*. Do I hear your cry in poems? Like Newlove's "The Weather," tears are just another word for love. Like you, like memory. But we sat once on your front step in that last spring with the first bulbs blooming – snowdrops, crocus, daffodils – and talked about poems, how much we loved Neruda, Sexton, Plath, and how, if you got a grant, you'd leave him. You stayed and stayed and stayed. A hammer! Christ. I try to imagine it and fail away at the image, him crushing your skull then dumping you naked in Furry Creek. What could have been in his mind as he took your clothes off, the body in his hands one he had loved. It's all suburbs now, a road leading to Whistler, and there's no plaque or bench by the creek to honour you. I go round and round, your bad teeth, your poverty, your children, that man running down the hall with his head a battering ram striking the wall and you putting down the phone and going to him, perhaps holding him in your long arms, cradling his hurt head in your lap and whispering to him that it was okay, that you had him now, that you loved him, really loved him. Was that how it went? Or did you throw him a rag and walk away? No, you never walked away. There's a white stone in my shade garden. It's a crooked one, a single piece of shattered quartz. It glows in the night, the stars giving just enough light. Bright stone. It will make me think of you when I walk the mottled path under the cedar. It's a pebble path pretending to be water. Each time I look at it I think of your body, the wild creek crashing down from the mountains and your white body in a pool, a single steelhead fingerling swimming through your fingers, another touching your lips and me in the dark under the trees, wondering at the silence that is the story of men. They put an arbutus on the cover of your last book, Pat, the bark peeling from the tree as if scraped by the sun. It's a tree that only lives where water hides away. It's why you can't transplant them from the wild. Their roots go on forever even as they lose their skin. I'm sorry I almost forgot you. The years for me get gathered crookedly. I remember only what I can. I keep lists of what I need to remember: I must buy milk and bread today, work in the garden while the sun shines, feed the cats, place flowers by my woman's bath, talk to a friend, write a poem. If I call you, will there be an answer?

FOR IRVING LAYTON

1.

Maybe this letter is dead. I know you're not, but I expect to hear you're
gone each time the day arrives. It's the stumble light makes, faces reach-
ing out to us in the dark. We call it waking up, unsure who we are in the
false dawn. The older I get the more confused I am. Dying seems such
a simple thing. I'm amazed it takes most of us so long to get it right.
You live in time and the dead start to accumulate. They're like trees I
used to see in spring up the North Thompson when the ice went out,
the ones whose roots gave way to water. Their falling was so long and
slow, all whisper going down. And then their rolling into the hook above
Mad River where the rocks were. The trees hung up there, their bodies
for a season green among a hundred years of trees. Strange how fir and
spruce turn white from water. They're like the thoughts the canyon has,
things beaten to the colour of old bone. Fear makes us brave, Irving. I'm
not afraid anymore. The dark is just the need to make something out
of nothing. There are questions I could ask, but like old Socrates, they
always lead to a kind of foolishness: *ambition, pride, the ecstasy of sex*,
lists that make no sense. Just words. Old Nietzsche had it almost right,
the part where the poet walks a wire above the street. I always thought
it best to walk those wires in the dark. Seeing things have always made
me fall. It's your snake keeps coming back to me, its *last silent scream*.
I'd seen the same in the hills above the lakes, seen the wisps of grass in
its mouth, the twists and turns of pain. I killed the first rattlesnake I saw,
thinking its suffering made easier by death. But that's the thing a young
man does to hide his fear. I know I'll pay for that death after I'm dead. Is
that what transformation is? Tell me if you know. I'm weary these days.
There's a riddle in my skull and I was never good at riddles. Being born
is enough to make a man wonder what a meaning is. Maybe that's why
I keep writing poems. This letter like all the rest is full of questions. I'd
send this to you but what good would that do? I remember having coffee
with you in '68 up The Main while you talked about poetry. I didn't say

a word. Young men don't speak to heroes, especially the ones who talk of freedom in a poem. You and Yeats on your stilts. I keep trying not to lie, imagine butterflies and Buddhas, twist and turn. You're not dead and so my grief is greater. The dead are breathless swimmers. Remember that night at York? Eli was talking poetry while you kept trying to get that girl to go to the hotel with you. You never got the girl. I did later, but I never told you. I loved your trying though and want to say she was as marvel-ous as you imagined. Such breasts she had, such thighs. I was just young enough to interest her lust, that's all. But Irving, you showed a way for me to write myself toward a paradise and though I never got there, still, it was all in the reaching. I too have wanted to sing *in the throat of a robin*. And though it is a furious path where black dogs howl I walk it anyway. You told me that. I think you'd tell me now if you could speak. The gods aren't dead, not yet, though their bodies lie in the huge rivers, stripped of their flesh, while all about them is the great noise of the waters as they take whatever they can reach to a darker sea.

2.

I went out to Maimonides to see you after I wrote that poem. In the hall I got confused and couldn't find your room. I turned to a group of people sitting in easy chairs. They were watching television with the sound turned off. I asked them where I was going and they all turned at my voice with the looks of the demented and deranged. Such smiles they had. A little ashamed and confused I shrugged and stepped away. One old lady waved at me. There was no *waterfall of grief* in her, just a simple joy at being asked anything. Like Jarrell's cry of *Change me*, I saw what I might be and so waved back, a little foolish, a little less ashamed. You were in the room in your chair, staring through your window, intent on Montreal, just houses and apartment blocks, streets and cars blinking through the rain. There were photographs on the tables and on the walls, you with Leonard, and you with your mother, a picture taken years ago when you were still your mother's son. You didn't look at me, just sat there staring at that pane of glass between you and whatever world there was. I picked up your book and it opened to your poem, the one I loved when I was young. I remember promising myself that poem back in the sixties and swore I'd never lie, but like all poets I failed at truth, thinking rhetoric an easier disguise. How quiet whispers are. I told you I loved you. You just raised your hand to your lips and stroked a knuckle across the place where words get made. They told me your skull still holds your body alive. You don't speak anymore, your poems all in your head. There must be such beauty there. I read to you the words that started me down this long road of poetry. You said the death of your father sent you toward what you feared most. In the end we all touch a knuckle to our lips. I made a whisper of your poems. That was enough. In the hall outside I waved to the woman in the chair. She stared at me. She had the look I've seen on every broken thing I've touched, querulous, her hands asking me who I was, palms out, the name of what kept hurting her, the sound turned off, the images flickering just beyond her eyes.

PART TWO

UNDER THE SUN IN THE DRY DESERT HILLS
WHERE THE RAIN NEVER FALLS IN AUGUST

In deep sand a beetle shoulders her way toward paradise.
A sunflower, wild with yellow, covers her with one shadow.
Among the grains of quartz, one bruised garnet, a cone of pine.
The beetle clambers. There is nothing like her in the world.
Almost blind, I get down on my knees.
My bare feet have the same soles they had when I was born.
My mother is dead.
Among many things I am alive. Still.
A single drop of water falls.
The beetle stops for a moment, but she does not drink from the salt.
There is somewhere she has to go and she goes on.
Mightily.

FORMS

Decline, the way
things slope, lessen,
there, the angle of
the scree, things
held in place, a note,
a diminution, as of
the breath, what
builds from what
fails, fallen, what
bends under, what
gives way, diminished,
as the dying do,
the lessening, as of
last days, limbs
moving more
slowly, a decay,
without violence,
the mountain
revealing what
light I could
not see, abated,
abandoned to
this fallen stone
at rest, inclined,
unearthed.

THE SHRINE

You think of the boy opening the casket in his father's bedroom,
the one where he kept his regalia from The Shrine and wonder
at what secret he desired, as if secrets were all buried
things, an archeology of love he dug for, holding up the apron
with its scimitar and star, the scrolled Aramaic text that told him
nothing, the books with their ritual responses, what he does not
remember now. Like all things of his father's, they were a mystery.
He'd heard his father memorizing pages of text,
the mutter of his tongue going over and over the arcane lines
he needed to repeat to the circle of men down at the temple
The fictions of his father were many, all hidden, so a boy,
crying out for the story was given only shards, bits of broken clay
in the till that was his father's living. Death was far away. The boy
had no thought of that, living as he did in his immortal flesh.
To the boy it was as if his father's mind were a broken thing
and what spilled out were only shattered pieces, things
an archeologist might have put together to display
in a locked, wooden case where a boy might hover and imagine
this fragment of wood, papyrus, vellum,
bits of goat skin that revealed nothing but an image,
a mysterious verb that told him to run and hide, a bird's head
that might have been a hawk, some raptor made into a god
to guide the dead to that other world.

TEACHING POETRY

Certainty, fidelity
On the stroke of midnight pass
Like vibrations of a bell . . .
Giving her three lines of "Lullaby," and wanting
her to hear the bells in the first line,
knowing she must come to it alone or not at all,
walking after in the Nitobi Garden alone,
having to place my feet carefully on the stones
leading down to the water, the last stone
where I stopped and looked out upon the world,
water leading to water and the trees above,
their leaves, koi showing their backs to the sun,
thinking what I know now is what I didn't know
back then, buried as I was in *Job*
and *Ecclesiastes*. Just eighteen, I lay beside
my first wife and read aloud to her from the Bible
those old words from centuries ago. High school nights,
my first child inside her, my son, who hasn't spoken
to me for twelve years now. This stone, that stone,
my student who's reading Auden's poem and is
or is not hearing the bells in that first line, old
hearts, that certainty, the bells.

SEVENTEEN ROADS OUT AND CHOOSING

At the edge of the mountain road a toad crouches beside a yellow stone.
The pool of mud and water tells me nothing of my daughter.
I'm cold and wonder is not told by what I say.
I pray for what I know.
Somewhere in the rain my daughter stares through light.
I imagine her, slight and still, quietly.
Beyond the road, the fronds of sword ferns droop down below death camas,
a mound of white froth. What I see, I've lost.
The solitary toad squats like old leather beside his stone.
The road has no daughter. Here at the edge I pledge what I have to her.
Here, I say, *here*, knowing I pray for little, a pool of water,
yellow stone, a toad, my daughter in the first of dawn,
far from this place at the edge of her careful lawn.

A CUP OF STONE

Water leaves its mark on stone. What falls
moves mountains. In the mines my father
worked in the great darkness of stones,
bringing from the belly of the earth
silver for the wrists and necks of women
in the far cities. The quartz he sucked
into his lungs hissed with each breath
he took, so that laying my head
on his breast I thought his ribs held
in their cage a crystal chime. His death
was another kind of mountain. His life
was the measure I made from time,
so like a stone whose belly is hollowed
by falling water, the sound in the empty
mine shafts where he laboured is what I hear
when I place my ear against his earth.
A cup of stone. I have seen everything
and I have done nothing in this world.
There are days I want to kill my mind:
the woman who leans toward her man,
her necklace making the softest sound,
as silver does against silver, as water
does when it touches hollow stone.

NOT GOING TO THE NITOBI GARDEN, CHOOSING POETRY INSTEAD

In the white coffee mug a yellow flower, nameless,
picked at dawn, her sleeping in the muscled dark, bright hair
thick with sweat. Him sitting in the wicker chair, silent,
staring at the flower with the old regret. A wasp
rages at the window, the glass between its wings and paradise.
It crashes its helmet head against what can't be reached, cedar trees,
magnolias, penstemon, and the last blooms of the foxgloves.
In the redwood tree a grey brain thinks among the branches,
a wasp nest where eggs lie in cells, each one a thought, each one
what he can only imagine. He doesn't open the window,
wonders instead at her dream, the click of the wasp's blunt head on glass,
what she's translating now, what dream of hell she holds,
the *click, click* . . . *click, click* of the wasp, and her shifting,
the hair falling across her cheek. All this and waiting,
the wasp in fury on the flower, the only thing
resembling, nectar pooled below, the flower still
alive in spite of its death, and her waking, slow to morning,
him in the wicker chair, its brittleness creaking, and
not going to her, the wasp under its bright wings, watching.

MINIATURE

A man sleeps in a chair by the wall, his bare feet out
on knotted pine grown dark with time, the left one
with its bit of blood hooked carefully over the right.
The quiet light in the room is pale, reflected
off the blue hills to the east. In the corner
a woman patches the worn heel of a sock.
Through the thin strands of worn wool a china egg
glints like the single eye of a bird at twilight.
Her hands slide the darning needle in and out.
It seems to be flying there, a small whisper
like the bird inside. The day is almost gone
and she squints to see what her hands are doing.
They know their way.
The sock she is darning is one of a thousand, thousand socks
she's mended in her life.
In a moment she will wake him.
The sock is almost done. His workboots – the leather worn away
on the toes so that the steel plate shows – sit side by side,
placed carefully as if the man might leap into them
and move stunned to the door
to find what lies beyond in the coming night.
We're sure we've been here before, the story
an old one of a man in a chair, a man
who has worn the socks she mends. We know
he will wake and step out into the night.
She waits, her hands moving in a silence
broken only by the clicks of the needle
against the darning egg. We're sure.
There is her breathing, her small bird-like chest
rising and falling, the man in his chair, the needle moving
with its sharp beak so much like death's sharp snout,

the tip of it blackened because it was heated by a sulphur
match only an hour ago to sterilize it before she took out
the wooden shard from his left heel. It's what
she waits for now, his leaving. Death's sharp snout,
yes, that's what we're seeing, a little bird of death coursing
over the egg under her hands. In and out, the steel beak
flies as the light, almost without regret, waits quietly away.

THE SOOKE POTHOLES

A tree frog's creak and croak are all that beauty is
when we're alone. Sometimes a song is all we have.
And the water swirls in the potholes down in the canyon.
The people are gone home to bed and I'm sitting on a stone
at the forest's edge listening to a tree frog's only song.
Out here in the dark alone I think of my woman.
A saw-whet owl calls from the other side of the canyon.
The frog answers back, happy there's someone he can talk to.
Above me the moon holds onto her bright daughter.
She wants to fly away from here, her curved arms wings of light.
I came to hold what is left of the wild and found
a blouse, a running shoe, and the torn cover of a book called
Natural History. But there's nothing natural about history.
I listen to the waters.
They say they've travelled far to find this place.
I say little, having little to say.
The waters go on to the ocean, busy,
happy to find the place where it all began. I think water
knows more than I of love. Old Hugh Latimer back in 1549
told his king, *The drop of rain maketh a hole in the stone,*
not by violence, but by oft falling.
Sometimes a gentle soul is what we want.
What can be saved, I ask, but the moon and the stars,
the owl and the frog tell me nothing of salvation.
If my woman were here she'd say all will be well,
knowing I need love at times a little.
Her song saves me tonight, no matter love.
She tells me there are living things.
I listen to the waters far below, the scour of stone on stone.
Like the tree frog's song, I think the earth is singing.
The owl knows he will starve if he waits for the mouse

to crawl under his talon, and the tree frog knows
no lovely frog will come without a song.
Nor pray for tree nor frog nor man,
but praise that *we* are a living place,
the whisper of these waters ours to hold,
however brief our stay.

LOOKOUT

Sometimes you look out over the great plains
and see a faint light falling between what we think are mountains.
It is then you know you are living far away from the world.
As the abandoned hulk of a turtle you found once in a field
far from water. How you squatted on your bare heels and stared at the bulk
of that green dome. The body a thought inside that emptiness.
Or the night you stood by the redwood tree on the street outside your home
and stared through the burden of heavy needles at your wife
as she stared out of the light. How for one moment you were afraid.
Sometimes we live far away from the world,
bright sunlight, a heavy dark. Without thought, and waiting.

TWO CROWS IN WINTER

Two crows on the fir tree after days of rain.
They click beaks, lean to each other, blue shoulders touching.
They preen the blades of their wings, the long stretch of hollow bones
the arch they hang their feathers from.
The sun glints from their sleek heads, little servants of war
whose life is the fallen, the forgotten.
One drops to the street and returns with the body of a dead rat,
so small, the thin tail hanging like a dropped thread.
The other cowls and rolls its head, bright eye to the sun.
It leans its cheek against the wet fur,
its beak cleaning the skull of its last thought.
They are in no hurry to eat.
The day is longer than the night, the rare sun a blessing,
the rat a later meal, a death to share in some other, farther tree.
Their wings break as the sun holds their blue.
They fall beyond my sight as I, as if in prayer, bend
down, returning my hands to the earth.

AUGUST LIGHT

White sand and the gold running deep in the sun
at the far bend where a spring run jammed the wrack,
branches and leaves, an old tire, and a bit of cloth caught up
like a sail flung hard against still air, the bed of the creek deep
where no wind moved. The path did not wander. It followed
the land of Mississippi, each footfall as much animal as man,
around the hill, not over, stump and root, rock and hump
as distance, not discovery. This way, the worn bridge
over the creek old, the boards ground grey and curved
by foot and paw, hoof and claw, how many years, and how
many bridges over this dry creek and through this forest,
the path one path so one could in the oldest days
follow them from the north to the south or east to west,
an intricate map that covered a continent – so long ago,
as I, moving south of the Nechako, followed the trails
through the mountains to the Cariboo plateau
I sat there in the forest looking down upon
the first man I had seen in a month and didn't move,
bushed, on my haunches behind tamarack needles,
my rifle butt on a stone, and watching him
as he moved from barn to house to truck and down
the road away and how I slipped back into the trees
for three more days, my fire small in the night, thinking
my way back into being a man again. The last night
I brewed coffee in the pot while a Blue grouse baked in clay.
Broken open, the meat of the bird I thanked the land for.
And now this old creek bed, deep and waterless, white sand,
and going on through the wood behind Faulkner's Rowan Oak,
and onto Oxford in this far Mississippi I never thought
I'd see. I'd read *Light in August* in the hotel
and found the creek in his book exactly as it was,

the trail he took from town to home and back again how many
times? And the time I sat behind green limbs
and watched another of my kind, quiet for three days,
thinking by the fire that I might kill someone and not
knowing whom. That man I was followed a path southwest
leading him I knew, even as he wished to be lost, back to himself,
the Cariboo, late August light. I
stare at the sand shot with gold in Faulkner's dry creek bed,
each journey old as the trails that lead us again to the world.

BILLIARDS

Light approaches from the east and I go out into the dark, wanting, a late raccoon scrambling over the fence, surprised by me or just in a hurry, a beetle in his mouth. Something about fear. As if there was a way to explain sound in the garden larger than a chickadee worrying the carapace of a sunflower seed.

And then she died, well, and that was the end, the nurse pulling the curtains and then an orderly trundling her body out. I heard the rubber wheels, one of them bent or twisted so it rattled as it went, skittering like a grocery cart on the polished floor, the curtain in the way of my sight, the room, white. I sat there and thought it was deliberately painted that colour because death could be better seen against its light or that light becomes us in the extreme, like the blonde hair of an early lover, someone young, and she, abashed, shy, but with desire, did what?

Yes, and the light caught in her hair, almost white, as was hers though she was old and the hair, thin, flared against her skin, the scalp freckled, and I thought of islands—the other, light in her blonde hair, I didn't think, after, astonished at what my body had done, could do.

To my left a Kodiak bear, harlequin duck and a bull moose argue about how much I'm willing to salve my guilt over a wilderness that isn't there, not anymore. Some wilderness committee sending me notepaper with their visages staring out. Mute testimony like the poems I write in my sleep, my wife turning me over when I cry out.

So the man whose mother had just died sat in the chair in the corner of the hospital room and waited for them to pull the curtain back and when the orderly did the bed was empty. It was like what a magician had done back when he was a boy, a showman who vanished a blonde girl on a stage in a high mountain valley-town in the old days. A place where a moose would sometimes walk down Main Street. The men in the bars and on the carved granite post-office steps would talk about such a visitation late at night over their last beers, saying, *Imagine that*, and sometimes, when there was a silence, Old Jimmy, the blind guy from Salmon Arm would say, *Can you imagine?*

And you can't.

When the blonde girl vanished up there on the stage, my father said to my mother, *I'll be go to hell.* Smoke and mirrors, girls vanishing, a moose on Main Street, that blonde girl when I was not yet a man, standing there in her panties, arms crossed upon her breasts.

I go outside and take a small broom to the meditation garden and begin sweeping the redwood needles away. The raccoon that scrambled over the fence stopped long enough to take a shit on the Zenigata stone and I wipe it away with a bit of moss and then sit on the cedar stump and sip warm coffee. I think about maybe going back in to finish a story, my cat Roxy watching me from the safety of the porch, she having been found down by the docks, a feral kitten, the others dead except for one male, her brother, and her mother dead too, Roxy at four weeks suckling on her brother's tiny penis, and now five years old, careful, still not trusting that I will let her back into the house, sure I will take her back to the docks down at the harbour where the rats are, and me going back into the house, Roxy crowding through the door and then hiding for a moment under the dining room table as she always does. Staring out.

My mother looked up from her deathbed and I did not know who she saw, perhaps a shadow only, something between her and the sun.

The cat made no move until I sat down in my chair. Only then did she come out from hiding, belly low to the floor, not crawling, but as a cat does, as if without legs, as the old comics used to do or Russian or Ukrainian dancers in their skirts in a half-squat scuttling across the stage, the cat, like that, moving.

As much desperation as discipline, I said, and my wife told me to write that down or else I would forget it and I got pen and paper and sat back down and asked her to tell me what it was I had said, my mind between the couch and the telephone stand, having gotten lost entirely as it seems to do the older I get and writing it down, folding the scrap of paper and stuffing it in the back pocket of my jeans.

If you don't use it, I will.

I look out the window and a redwood frond, pale red, falls from a branch into the pool of water in the hollowed stone.

Desperation, and that got me going.

When I was still a boy I married a girl and she gave birth to a son, and I sat by her bed in the hospital after the birth I had not been allowed to watch or even be near, the nurses telling me to go away and only come back when it was all over, the *it* being something I didn't want to think about, happy a decision had been made that excluded me because I had not wanted to be there anyway, and she, my wife, the girl I'd married in high school, was afraid – and the story, because fear is at the heart of every story, the unknown always just ahead, was about an old man who had come into the ward, made his demands and had made love, no, *fucked* his young wife, the girl in the bed beside my wife, the girl saying, *No, no, no.* It was just after the woman had given birth. And me, a boy, looked at my wife, what was she, barely eighteen years old, her blonde hair streaked with sweat, and frail after twenty-nine hours of labour, crying, telling me of this, and I, also eighteen, afraid of her story and knowing that somehow her telling me meant I had to do something about it, looking across the bed to the other bed where the girl, younger than my wife, who had been raped by her husband, lay staring at the ceiling, and I had been afraid as she told me what had happened and, strangely, excited by her story, my wife weeping, and me suddenly hard in my pants, ashamed and afraid, asking for details as if by her giving them to me I could, in her eyes, know more and so somehow better able to do something about what had happened, but also wanting to hear more of what the man had done and how he'd done it, *What did she say?* And, *What did he do then?* And loving my new wife, this girl, our son who I hadn't seen yet, somewhere else in the hospital being washed and cleaned and checked out by the doctor or whoever it was had taken him away . . .

The ellipsis which is railed against, that moment in Romance novels when the girl with the blonde hair, almost white, steps out of her panties and stands naked as he moves toward her, dot, dot, dot, etc., the black boots, the quirt he slaps against his leg, his thick hair tumbling across his forehead, dot, dot, dot.

Oh, tell someone walking down Mission Hill, a father now, looking for a game at the pool hall, my friends all still in school writing final exams that would take them away somewhere, to university or college, or just to some good job somewhere, and no one in the pool hall except Paul Rivard staring across the scratched glass countertop, dust in the air, a Tuesday, my boy's life refusing to end, some other life beginning, and like all the old stories, ending, *kind of*, as in kindness, or the right kind, the word so strange suddenly, I write it down again, *kind*, as if it might help explain anyone's tears, and telling no one, of course, of my jerking off in the pool hall toilet, ashamed, wiping myself, and then shooting balls around the table, practising bank shots, a billiard game for one, Paul telling me how to use the carom and how to keep the balls clustered in one place on the table, working them against each other until I had to leave the cue ball safe for the invisible man I was playing against, there being no one there but myself.

The raccoon turns the beetle over and over in his paws, as if it was a bright jewel or as the frog in that poem translated from Ghengis Khan's time and which a friend used in a poem: *O frog, jewel of the water.* And staring at the raccoon staring at the moon's light in the shining disc of the beetle's shell, such wonder, that bright bauble, that fragile testimony.

Pale light through the windows. It fell upon the white floor, a living thing come from the night, the moon a far wandering. I watched it become thinner and thinner, a curved blade diminishing, the shadow of its other body a weight only the sky could hold. Swollen, it obliterated the stars as it passed to the mountains of the west, a dark belly held in arms of light.

I remember my mother holding her belly the same way when she carried her last child, my brother, five years after the war. I saw her standing back from the wringer washing machine, the piles of clean and dirty clothes on the slat bench, clasping her hands below her as if holding a stone. I watched her from the porch door and saw what was a mother, mine.

Like that, her tiredness; like those, her days.

The hours don't exist.

I lift her out of the past. Her bones are potsherds found in a till, fragments of time plowed under.

In the hospital room the only measure was her breath. Her hair was a fall of grey on the pillow, the colour of a heron's breast at dawn above the tide. I had come to be with her in death. There had been others die before her, too many, my brother with his skull full of blood crying crazy in his bed, the drowned girl I found in the run-off waters of the Nicola River, her body tangled in a net of roots and branches, cutthroat trout lilting in her hair, the old remittance man I helped bury up the North Thompson. I was barely a man back then, the backhoe gouging the grave he would lie in, unnamed, unmarked, forgotten but for my going back years later and laying a stone where I thought his bones might be, thinking apology a remedy for grief.

Who can be forgiven?

My murdered father?

My Uncle Jack pushed me bodily into his coffin as he shouted at me, *Kiss him! Kiss your father goodbye!* It was the first I knew of love between men, Jack's tears, my struggle, the lipstick and powder on my father's face marking me, I think, forever.

And there were other deaths before, but what do they matter to me who watched his mother fail away? I'd seen the old ones walking in the park outside the hospital. They passed by with such slowness I could see through them to the trees and the towers of the city. The ocean's light turned them diaphanous, thin mist their shroud, bowed heads and tentative steps the measure of the lives they'd lost, the last to fail themselves. Once I reached out as if to touch a woman's hand and she stopped a moment and looked at me, O, from such a distance. No, not a stranger's hand, my mother's, and she rocked her head a moment as if to wonder who I was. I touched her hand and helped her back to the bench and sat her down.

What's wrong with you?

Her question old as life. A few weeks before she vanished, thin smoke, a mist rising.

A woman's hand, my mother's.

Who am I that I should write now of her death who carried me gentle in the waters of her womb? Too long ago to tell and today I'm older than my father and in ten years I'll be older than her and I'll know less and less until at last I'll know nothing, nothing at all. What did she know who blessed me at the end?

Blessing, warning?

Grief is a deep well. We dive into those waters until we become the rings that radiate from us, pale circles vanishing. I circle my grief like the poet said of his mother, *quietly*.

Years ago I watched a tidings of magpies surround a young gopher come early from his burrow. Unlike the old ones he didn't know to sleep through the cold and restless rose to the earth and the betrayal of the winter sun. The magpies trapped him outside his burrow. There were seven birds or nine, some uneven number, and they sported with the gopher. Confused, he seemed not to know why they held him there. Each time he tried to get to the safety of its burrow one or another of the birds would peck and drive him back.

Such play was theirs. I couldn't stay to watch the death and I didn't drive the birds away. Surely I am like that tidings of magpies. I won't let go what I hold. I play with it, my life a two-sided coin in a magician's hands. It seems at times I play with death.

I'm weightless, grief itself.

The last night before she slept she put her makeup on. At first I thought she'd become so deluded she didn't know if she was going to sleep or waking up and then I knew she was making herself beautiful. She'd told me she couldn't wait. *I'll be with your father*, she said. *Your brother, too*. A lipstick slash across her lips, her hand trembling so she smeared it cross her cheek. And her hair. She had so little, just a few spare strands, yet she combed them carefully down over her forehead, brightly, sprightly, as she had all her life. Women and their hair. And rouge too on her cheeks, too much, but I knew her eyes had failed. What she saw in the tiny mirror I held up was a face as young and beautiful as she thought she'd always been.

As she was and would be.

Death eats us alive. I could see her skull. It was such a fragile thing, that bone cup I think held who she was. There was a time in the far past when people thought the soul lived in the groin and then they imagined it the heart. When did we decide upon the skull as a container for the soul? How far away from our bodies can we go until we lose sight of ourselves and think our souls reside outside us or don't reside at all?

Who did I see lying on the bed in that hospital room where the last light of the moon shone pale through the window? What does a mother know when a child resides in her? Is there a moment when the soul arrives? Does a mother place her hands on her still-flat belly and feel through her palms that first arrival? To have a soul within a soul?

What does a man know?

I feel at times a man balanced on canes at the edge of a park, some shriven, reckless thing, someone last, lost, left behind. One day I watched an old one in the park. He stood by the far trees and like the trees he swayed with the wind come off the sea. It wasn't a heavy wind, just some light touch of air come weaving. He was still there when I left to go back inside the hospital and I wondered as I walked away if anyone knew he was there, if anyone was going to come and take him to wherever he was to go. Perhaps he saw around him angels in the shapes of magpies, a tidings of things to touch him to his rest.

I wish my father had lived long enough to die.

I wish my mother had my father longer.

But what are wishes but luck gone wanting? I seem to begin everything with a question. Perhaps there are only questions. But there must be more? Surely there's only a presence of things for lack of thinking farther than I can. Back then I lost what lay before me, but what made me think she was mine to lose?

I am bewildered.

A year before her death I went into the mountains to lose myself. I walked back into the bush until the hills became rocks, the creeks thin rivulets born from the fingers of glaciers as they retreated through tumbled scree. There were no trails but for bear and mountain goat. I sat at the beginning of water. I saw the birth of rivers rise in the far mountains. I knelt on the ground and leaned my face into first water and I drank from a clear pool, took into my body what once was snow.

I'm made at times of ice.

I camped by a nameless creek and made my fire. I lay myself down on pine boughs under the stars and thought I was the only man there was, I was that lonely. There were so many stars I thought there must be a god for what else could have caused them to flare so willingly. I think I'm that old man in the park.

The other women in the ward were far away in sleep. My mother was awake. We didn't speak. Her bright eyes stared at me, curious. She had a quizzical look, the kind that wonders. What do the dying see? On my knees was *The Old Curiosity Shop*. I brought it thinking it was her favourite of his books. She loved Dickens. She'd read him aloud to me and my brothers when we were children: *A Tale of Two Cities, Bleak House, Hard Times,* the rest. We lived those pages of the far past, that other, older century, the nineteenth after Christ. She revelled in words, loved the detail of a world that was still in reach when she was but a child.

Who was she back in the days of the little girls?

I remember what she was like when I was a boy. The time she clasped her hands under her belly in the kitchen when she stepped back from the washing machine and the tubs and held her last, my brother a stone in her arms. What did she think as she held his body in herself? Why can I see her?

She was tired of her sixteen-hour days and nights of looking after a family on little money, a wood stove, a laundry tub for baths, linoleum on the floor curled at the edges where it met the walls and worn away under the pine table where we sat to eat the food she made.

She paused for breath.

I don't remember her laughing. The only thing she would smile for was a camera and that was a thin smile, deceptive in its slight. It was as if she knew something the rest of us didn't. She had a magpie look, curious and playful, strangely, cruelly kind.

She closed her eyes when I read to her. The woman across from her never moved. She'd been in a coma a long time. The ward cat slept in the hollow of her legs and stared at my mother and me. I didn't look back. I wrote a poem the night her husband slept with her.

> The man in the hospital who, late
> in the night, the women, sick, asleep,
> took off his clothes, folding them neatly
> and laying them down, the shirt and pants,
> the socks and underwear, and the shoes
> side by side beside the white chrome chair,
> in a room with only a small light
> burning above each bed, lifted
> the covers and lay down
> beside his wife who had not wakened
> for two years from the coma, and

placing his arm across her breasts,
his leg upon her leg, closed his eyes,
silent, still, the breathing of his wife,
his arm rising and falling with her life
while the ward cat who would sleep
with only her, watched from
the foot of the bed, one ear forward
and the other
turned to the sounds of the distant city.

I looked at that woman on her bed. She had no visitors I saw but him that
once. I think she was alone and whatever family there was had given up
on her. That man said nothing to me, so intent he was on love. It seemed
I wasn't there at all. The ward cat knew. Like the cat was the old woman
in her sleep. Like a magpie my mother. Like that man am I.

I'm sick to death of death. There was a time a man would hire wom-
en to wail for him. They'd come in their long dresses and black shawls
and sit in a circle. They'd sit and knit, talk among themselves as women
do, but when death came they'd rise up and howl as if with their bod-
ies they could cry all grief away. Is that what death is, some god come
calling? Where were such women that I might have hired them? Would
they be called a grief of women in the way magpies are a tidings, crows
a murder, orphans an abandonment? Is this what I do here, list things in
their gatherings?

I'm sick of me.

I remember the night I left the bar at the Cecil Hotel. It was three
years after my father's death, three years after the poets had deserted
the place at the end of the sixties and the Cecil became a country-and-
western bar with strippers and pole-dancers, addicts and drunks, pimps
and johns and whores. I was drunk and stoned and tired of booze and
whores. I walked down to False Creek where the ocean never moved. It's
odd to think how I folded my clothes and placed them on a rock. How
neat I was. I sank a dozen times and each time my body rose again to

the surface, refusing to let go of its hold on things. I sank again and then again, each time thinking this was surely the last. At the end I lay on my back upon the water and stared up at the stars.

Death doesn't come to us easy. It's us who must come to death. We're welcome then.

I think my mother was welcome.

I think she was good at death who wasn't good at life. Why do I say that? God knows, she gave birth to us three and raised us through the war and then two more, my sister, my little brother.

I saw her hold her belly in her arms as if her last was what she must endure. There were no more. Old Doctor Alexander cleaned her out. He promised her that when she asked for an abortion. *You have this one and I'll make sure you have no more.* I can hear him talking quietly in the kitchen. I was at the porch door listening. I think at times I was some kind of ghost child, a spirit sent to keep close watch on her. She never told my father what she did. Five was enough and she was tired of birth. He came hard, my brother, born at the end like that. Eleven pounds he was. She told me he split her open when he came. *He almost killed me,* she said.

I read to her there in the night. The past came stuttering, glimpses, bits and pieces of a film stitched together every which way. There's no order to me. There never was. I remember too much. I remember wishing my brain would die. I remember wishing as I read from Dickens, her eyes closed, her hair combed just right, the lipstick crooked on her lips, her breathing light. I reached out and placed my hand upon her breast and held it there. I felt the bone cage move. I swear her lips couldn't lift a feather. She was a whisper made of silk so strange as to be made by the ghosts of worms.

All of them came back to me. It was as if I watched the dreams she had. As if what was in her mind became mine and I could see back through the war to some other, earlier time, the thirties and twenties, her in a jangly dress, my father with his foot up on the running board of a Model-A Ford, a cigarette in his hand, a cigarette in hers, the two of them young and wild. And later, the Sullivan Mine and my father coming down the rocky trail to her, two children, me not born, not yet, her belly swollen. Did she stand alone and hold me like the crescent moon holds night? I swear I'll kill my sight.

She reared up from the bed and grabbed my wrist. Her tiny hand just skin stretched over bone, fine vellum pulled across thin sticks. Shining there, her eyes what the almost dead have, a bright and terrible burning, and she said to me as if to admonish, as if to warn me of my only life, as if to make of praise another kind of calling: *At every turn there's always something lovely!*

So I sit and hold onto what death knew and knowing gave to me that I might turn my life, to what? O, mother, who is it I mourn? Whose death did I wait for in that room? I'm alive in a kept silence and I turn and turn again upon your words and wait upon my wanting. You died and I have nothing here but words. I make of them a memory to you who sang to me and sing to me still, your voice as bright as the sharp points of the moon before it's gone, that blade of light that holds the heavens, crescent-shaped, like two arms holding on to what it knows, curved around a belly where a stranger grows.

HE ANSWERS THE YOUNG CRITIC WHO DEMANDS THAT HIS POEMS CHANGE, OFFERING THE BOY BLOOD AND TOMATOES IN HOPE THEY WILL BE ENOUGH

When the little boy lay bleeding from his temple
on the white kitchen table in the village shack
in the high mountains, the women kept washing
the clot away, their rags opening the wound.
The blood flowed, the boy's face bright
with the rose glint of his body starving. It was as if
he kept himself alive only to stop their hearts.
As if their wailing could keep him alive.
As if the knife of the moon making its sickle cut
in the wine inside the glasses the men raised up
to the night could stop their women's tears.
Back there in the mountains the river was huge
with ice, and the men in the night listened
to the lament as the women opened
again the wound of the boy who was steadily dying
in their care. All things proceed from such
attention and it is hard to be as hard as the young
when they admonish their elders. How difficult
it must be to ask the rust on the iron knife
to go back to the beauty of the blade in
its first fire? Surely dust is its own beauty.
It is the same as picking up a stone
from among the many myriad stones
by the river and holding it out to see
the lichens growing there. One white.
One red. They are eating each other.
It will take another five hundred years.
That is what the young critic wants,
I think, but what do I know

of such abstract wishes? Imagine
the loneliness in being just a man.
Or the boy on the table, how
I moved the women aside and stitched
the flesh to flesh, closing the wound, and then,
in the decorous dance a stranger must do,
drank wine with the old men on the porch, saying
nothing, their nodding as they filled my glass.
They were impressed labourers brought from Portugal
to work on the railway, the fallen moon,
the ice on the river, men and boys and blood.
None of us spoke of the women's singing.
They had heard it for many years and I, still
young, had nothing to say about such patience.
O yes, the boy brought me a bottle of good whiskey
a week later, something his father could ill afford.
The father could not bring it to me himself, shame,
pride, some kind of awkward love. I had refused
his money, you see, so he sent his son,
the one I stitched together in the shack. His mother,
she who had cleansed the wound over and over again,
bowed her head to me each time we passed on the road.
She didn't speak English, but in the late summer,
she brought me a basket of tomatoes she'd grown,
holding two of the fruits out to me, one in each hand, rich
and red, her hands worn from work, the steady
growing that is the lot of women who have laboured
beside their men for thousands of years
that their sons might live, blood and tomatoes,
a boy who followed me everywhere for the years
I was there in the North, as if with his presence
he could protect me from harm. As if it was that.

HOPE AND LOVE

The spider
weaves her web
in the window
at dawn.
The night has been
cold and she moves
slowly, filament
to filament,
drawing from
herself a cage
that is
beauty to me
and to her
her only life.
It is morning
and she
has caught
nothing for weeks.
This is her last
web and it has
nothing to do
with hope
or love, only
that she must
sit in the centre
of her making
and know that
what will feed
her is to come
or not come,
the sun

on the far flowers
and nothing
rising in the frost,
no sound among
the false blossoming
this cold, this
early spring.

BAMBOO SEEDS

A bamboo screen and the bamboo above, the long wands
above the stone bench reaching in the long dream of seeds
that will not come for a hundred years or more.
Pebbles lead from here to the pond and the koi.
Deep in the water their brightness rests.
They eat their bodies slowly, spring far away and the snows to come.
Hard rains break above the earth.
The koi are deep in their blood.
I saw in my father that last year how patience comes before death,
not after, just as I see through the bamboo leaves
the great death coming to this world, the bamboo wands flung outward,
thin leaves, and the koi below. So quiet.
I am without tears, older than my father.

AGAINST METAPHOR

He opened the book of a poet he loved in retreat, a man
who seemed to have spent his life almost afraid of everything,
love, life, sorrow, death, and how the man always approached
such themes like a small boy would, a kind of desperate
insecurity in the tone of the poems that always ended
with the man being somehow brave in spite of his fear,
like a small boy would who was forced to approach
something terrible and did, but at great cost to himself.
He thought the poet must be very attractive to women
because of his fragility and the sure beauty of his poems.
The man's poems were like an apple being peeled
very slowly with a knife. The knife had been honed
for hours on a stone like the one his father had once owned
and which he had lost in one of the many moves he had made,
He had been driving into the foothills
west of Fort MacLeod, Pincher Creek behind him. The farm
his father had run away from when he was thirteen was near there
but he had never tried to find it. Paradise, his father had called it,
ruefully, half in bitter jest, but he was right, there being nowhere
on earth as beautiful as those southern foothills. His woman was asleep
beside him, her face slack in the deep world no one knows of,
there being no one who has reported back from that place
except for dreams. He loved her sleeping.
To amuse himself he began to count
the houses and apartments he had lived in,
anywhere longer than a week or two,
places where he thought he'd lived.
Through the foothills and up into the Crowsnest Pass
past the town of Frank that had been buried under a slide
back in the thirties, and then beyond into the Rockies,
as she slept and he counted slowly and carefully, not wanting

to miss anywhere, his mind crossing and recrossing the continent
and when she woke he had reached the last place, the one
they had just left. Eighty-seven places, he told her.
She laughed in the tousled way women do
when they are not sure they are beautiful yet
and laughed again, serious, as she turned the mirror down
on the sun visor and touched her face. The last thing she did
was to run her slender fingers through her hair and then
shake it gently into place. Satisfied, she turned to him brightly
as women do when they are beautiful again, and said, *Really?*
Then, because she was no different than anyone else, she began
to count the places she had lived in her life, listing them out loud,
the place on Second Street in Swift Current, the rooms at university
she lived in when she was a student in Saskatoon, the other rooms
in a town called Glaslyn, somewhere in central Saskatchewan
when she was first married. There were only twenty-three places,
most of them when she lived with him,
and when she was finished she looked wistful and somehow
disappointed, as if there should have been more, not as many
as his, but more than just twenty-three. It was as if her life
had failed her in some strange way, then she brightened again,
for she was a woman and still is who never stays dark for long
except once when another woman threatened her life, a madwoman
the police warned away, but who started his wife on a dark
journey it took a year to recover from, but that was two years ago
and she was better now. He had listened to her counting out her life,
but he had only half listened, his mind still thinking of his life.
Later, at his mother's apartment in the Okanagan, his mother
had corrected his total, adding places he had lived when he was
a small child and had forgotten. That makes ninety-three, he said,
and his mother, not to be outdone, began counting the places
in her life and managed, of course, to beat the twenty-three
of his wife, which irked his wife.

When his mother realized, even by lying, she couldn't
beat his total of ninety-three, she said he was lying,
that no one had ever lived in ninety-three places,
at least no one in her family.
When they left that afternoon to drive to the coast
and their new life there in his ninety-fourth house, his wife
told him she didn't like his mother and he told her he knew that
and it was all right, because he didn't much like her either,
though he loved her, had always loved her. *Of course*, his wife said,
she's your mother, isn't she? She said it in the way women do
when they think men are being hard on women, that
it was all right for her not to like his mother, but if he didn't
then there was something suspect in it, something male.
She said: *You have to love her. She's your mother.*
And instead of taking what looked like bait on an argument hook
and telling his wife that he had said he loved his mother, of course,
who wouldn't, but that he'd only said he didn't like her, etc., etc.,
and instead just kept driving down into Merritt where he had
lived in four different places, all of them gone now, except
for the trailer park where he'd lived in a trailer, but the trailer
wasn't there anymore. He'd moved it up the North Thompson in 1960.
When he left he sold it to a logger
Who burned it down after his family left him.
It was a bad-luck trailer anyway,
he told his wife and she agreed, though she shook
her head at the trailer park. *If you lived here*, she said, *you were
trailer trash*, and they both laughed. Later on, up the Coquihalla
she fell asleep again and he'd continued on over the mountains
toward the new life they were making for themselves.
He'd forgotten all of that time until he opened the book
of the man whose poetry he loved. He was in retreat
and he was searching for something, anything to write about.
He had started a poem about humility because it was the subject

of the book the monks were being read at dinner, something written
about Hilaire Belloc, a writer he hadn't thought of in forty years,
but the poem he tried to write was pretentious
as any poem would be that started from the premise of humility.
But when he opened the book a mugo pine card fell out of it,
a bookmark he'd used once a year ago and he read
the identity tag he had used to mark the page of a poem
he loved. The tag read, *Pinus mugo Pumilio: A densely branched,*
broadly spreading evergreen shrub clothed in handsome,
dark green, needle-like foliage that tolerates a wide range
of soil conditions. Full to part sun for best results.
He thought of the poems in the book and how the man
who wrote them wrote as if he was almost afraid of everything,
his poems reading like an apple being peeled very slowly
by a sharp knife, the peel coming away slowly, revealing
the white flesh shot with veins of red, and he thought of how
his mother was dead now and how he'd loved her very much
all her life, even when she was bitter and old and angry at him,
he thought, yes, angry at him for being alive, as if somehow
he should have died like everyone she had loved, her first son,
her brother, her husband, her father, all her sisters, everyone,
and for her, at the moment whenever it seemed he was there
with her, him too, dead and better off because of it . . . *but*
better for whom? he thought, the words running out and not caring,
not wanting to go much further, and muttering, *ninety-five, ninety-five,*
to himself, as if somehow a number could explain anything
like mother-love, or a mugo pine; or a man whose poetry
he loved that he could barely read, and how it hurt so much to know
anyone who could keep going in spite of his fear, that almost-
afraid being worse than anything he could imagine, anything,
and now that he was at the end of the poem he began to hate
the apple and the knife and the way he had slipped into the poem
through metaphor, and how he was against metaphor these days

and wanted his poems to be clear of artifice, and how no matter
how hard he tried, it kept getting into his poems, and he thought
of going back and taking that part out, but thought that would
somehow betray the poem, his father climbing back in, and
his grandfather burying his father's mother under the caragana
back of the farmhouse, the place near Pincher Creek
he had never tried to find, and couldn't now
anyway, everyone long dead who might have given him
directions, anyone who might have shown him the way.

ATTENTION

How else, but the child in the ditch, so simple,
as she pushes a little wheel of lemon in the ruts,
the only wheel left from her carriage all of gold
that the stars shining see nothing of, so bright
their slow turning in the night. How delicate
she holds the yellow star between her fingers, the blossom
far away now, and the white seeds wet and gleaming
as they slip into the earth she leaves behind. How far
her journey in this small place she has made of her
riding, the horses plumed and lifting
their feathered hooves, the carriage all of gold,
and the barefoot girl in the shabby dress,
her gloved hand raised in farewell, as if
this was her leaving, a child going far away,
her two small fingers holding the yellow centre,
the wheel turning so delicate inside the image
she is, and how you are with her now
and so, by such attention, changed.

JOURNEYS AND RETURNS

Our lament makes the sand fleas dance.
Their tiny wings know a great secret.

PYGMY OWL

I think the moon
at the edge
where the limb
bends, quickens
night. My hunger
is for her. She is
unlike this owl
who, still, still
moves, the light
folding over
her wings: she
sings, a
dove note,
not mourning,
but only song
directed toward
who waits, with
me, the small
mole, mouse
and beetle, moon,
the limb bare
but for the cold
dark under her
bright wings,
the breath
I hold, I,
sudden, hear.

ACROSS THE STRAIT THIN CLOUDS
WHISPER ABOVE THE TREES

Across the strait thin clouds whisper above the trees.
There is no rain. A dark age comes on little white feet
and every silence we've imagined will be ours.
Sorrow and sorrow and sorrow will be ours.
Out of silence, woe upon woe.
The child in your arms will be taken from you.
She will be dashed upon stones.
So too the child of your child.
And will you give solace to the one who cries out?
And will you?
O, I have seen us in the hours, in the long nights.
We will walk with nothing in our arms.

LAST WATER SONG

It is not the water you tried to find when you were young.
That was the water that lost you.
You climbed trees to look and the water was there.
You walked on the earth and the water was nowhere.
That was the losing water.
This water is the finding water.
It is cloud searching water.
When you are old it comes down.
It stretches out on the earth.
It says follow this water.
First water is woman water.
The belly of woman has this song.
That water was the first learning song.
This water is the last learning song.
It is the cloud under the earth.
Now you climb down roots to find this water.
Now this tongue is a root.
Open this mouth in the earth.
Now sing this water song.
Now you are the last water.